SAM HOUSTON

Library of Congress Number: 87-24161

3 4 5 6 7 8 9   92

Library of Congress Cataloging in Publication Data

Gleiter, Jan, 1947-
    Sam Houston/Jan Gleiter and Kathleen Thompson.
    (Raintree stories)
    Summary: Recounts the story of the man who lived with the Cherokee Indians, served as an American soldier, and became involved in Texas politics.
    1. Houston, Sam, 1793-1863—Juvenile literature. 2. Texas—Governors—Biography—Juvenile literature. 3. Legislators—United States—Biography—Juvenile literature. 4. United States. Congress. Senate—Biography—Juvenile literature. [1. Houston, Sam, 1793-1863. 2. Governors.] I. Thompson, Kathleen. II. Title.
    F390.H84G57 1987   976.4′04′0924—dc19   [B]   [92]   87-24161
    ISBN 0-8172-2660-5 (lib. bdg.)
    ISBN 0-8172-2664-8 (softcover)

SAM HOUSTON

Jan Gleiter and Kathleen Thompson

Illustrated by Joel F. Naprstek

RAINTREE
STECK-VAUGHN
L I B R A R Y
A Division of Steck-Vaughn Company

My name is Sam Houston. I was born March 2, 1793, in Rockbridge County, Virginia, seven miles east of Lexington at a place known as Timber Ridge Church. On the day of my birth I would, many years afterwards, celebrate the birth of a new country. For it was on my birthday that Texas declared itself free and independent.

I did not start school until I was eight years old. And I didn't do much after I did start. I learned to read and write, and gained some idea of arithmetic. I doubt if I had gone to school six months in all when my father died. I was fourteen at the time.

My mother was left with the heavy burden of a large family. She had six sons and three daughters. She at once prepared to cross the Allegheny Mountains and find us a new home on the banks of the Tennessee River. Few of you can have any idea of the hardships such a heroine had to meet. I hope the day may come when our young authors will set themselves to work to find the unwritten legends of such heroism and adventure.

There was a school in that part of east Tennessee about this time, and I went to it for a while. I had two or three books, among them the *Iliad*, which I read so constantly that I could repeat it almost entirely from beginning to end. I was later put to work behind the counter of a general store. In no time at all, I ran away to the Cherokee Indians across the river.

I stood nearly six feet tall and was straight as an Indian. When my family came to me and asked me why I had left home, I said that I preferred tracking deer to measuring ribbon. And I said that I liked the wild liberty of the Indians better than obeying my own brothers. I told them to go home and leave me in peace.

I passed three years with my Indian friends. I spent a lot of time chasing deer through the forest with a speed little short of their own. I also played all those sports of the happy Indian boys. We often wandered along the banks of the streams, sheltered by the deep woods, just talking of many things. I was adopted by the tribe and given the name "the Raven."

And yet, this running wild among the Indians, sleeping on the ground, chasing wild game, living in the forests, and reading Homer's *Iliad* seemed a pretty strange business. Some people used to say that I would be a great Indian chief or die in a mad house or be governor of the state, for it was very certain that some dreadful thing would happen to me!

This wild life among the Indians lasted until I was eighteen. During my visits once or twice a year to my family, I bought clothes and many little things to use among the Indians. This left me with a debt which I was bound in honor to pay. I had no other choice but to leave my "dusky companions" and teach the children of "pale-faces."

It was no easy matter to obtain a school. But in a short time I had so many students I had to turn some away, even though I charged what was considered a huge price. Before, no schoolmaster had asked above six dollars per year. I thought that one who had graduated at an "Indian university" ought to price his knowledge higher. I raised the price to eight dollars—one-third to be paid in corn, one-third in cash, and one-third in cotton cloth of many colors, in which the "Indian professor" was dressed. I also wore my hair behind, in a snug braid, which I thought added somewhat to my looks. I was probably mistaken.

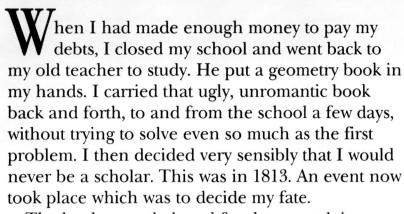

When I had made enough money to pay my debts, I closed my school and went back to my old teacher to study. He put a geometry book in my hands. I carried that ugly, unromantic book back and forth, to and from the school a few days, without trying to solve even so much as the first problem. I then decided very sensibly that I would never be a scholar. This was in 1813. An event now took place which was to decide my fate.

The bugle sounded, and for the second time, America was called to measure her strength against England. A recruiting party of the United States Army came to Maryville with music, a banner, and some well-dressed sergeants. Of course, I enlisted.

After a year of training, the Thirty-ninth Infantry took to the field to fight the Creek Indians, who had gone over to the British. General Andrew Jackson's army now had more than two thousand men, and his spies were scattered far and wide through the forests.

Retreating from village to village and point to point, the enemy had gathered on a bend of the Tallapoosa River. A thousand Indian warriors had taken their last stand.

It was in this battle that a barbed arrow went deep into my thigh. I kept my ground until my lieutenant and his men were by my side. I then called on my lieutenant to take out the arrow. The officer tried twice and failed.

"Try again," I said, my sword raised over my head, "and if you fail this time, I will strike you to the earth."

This time he drew out the arrow, tearing my leg as it came. A stream of blood rushed from the place, and I went to find the doctor to have the leg bandaged.

The years after the war I spent in the service of my state, my country, and General Andrew Jackson. I entered the office of Honorable James Trimble, who told me that with eighteen months of hard study I could become a lawyer. At the end of six months, I passed the examination. One year later, I was elected prosecuting attorney, making it necessary that I move to Nashville. One year after that, I was elected major general in the Tennessee Militia.

Not ten years after I began my study of law, I had been elected governor of the state of Tennessee. But again fate stepped in. My marriage to the lovely Eliza Allen ended in sadness and I felt that I must resign my office as governor. Because of the unfriendly acts of some people, I left Tennessee. I went to find comfort with my Indian father, Oo-loo-te-ka, the man the whites knew as John Jolly.

As I stood at the rail of my steamboat, I thought of the terrible unhappiness of my life. I thought, for an instant, that I would leap overboard and end my worthless life. At that moment, however, an eagle flew down on my head, and then, flying up with the wildest screams, was lost in the rays of the setting sun. I knew that a great future waited for me in the West.

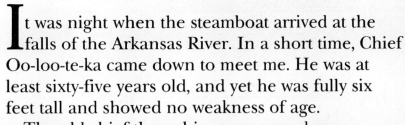

It was night when the steamboat arrived at the falls of the Arkansas River. In a short time, Chief Oo-loo-te-ka came down to meet me. He was at least sixty-five years old, and yet he was fully six feet tall and showed no weakness of age.

The old chief threw his arms around me.

"My son," said he, "eleven winters have passed since we met. My heart has often gone where you were. And I heard you were a great chief among your people. I heard that a dark cloud had fallen on the white path you were walking, and when it fell in your way, you turned your thoughts to my wigwam. I am glad of it. It was done by the Great Spirit.

"My people are in trouble, and the Great Spirit has sent you to us. I know you will be our friend, for our hearts are near to you. You will tell our sorrows to the great father, General Jackson."

When I laid myself down to sleep that night, I felt like a tired traveler who had returned at last to his father's house.

More years passed before I came to the land of my fate. In those days, I fought hard for the Indians, who were my friends and my family. I saw them cheated by the men who were chosen to protect them. When I tried to help them, I made enemies of my own people. At last, however, I found my way west. I found my way to Texas.

Texas was then ruled by Mexico. But there were many who wanted freedom. In new places, there are always noisy, second-rate men who want to make trouble. Texas was full of such men. And there seemed to be few who were brave, wise, and cool enough to deal with any trouble. Soon I was chosen commander-in-chief of the army of Texas.

In February of 1836, a letter was sent from a fort called the Alamo. It was signed by William B. Travis, and it was addressed to "the People of Texas and all the Americans in the world." It said that Travis and his men were surrounded by more than a thousand Mexican soldiers, led by Santa Anna. The Mexicans had said that any man who did not surrender would be killed. Travis had answered with a cannon shot.

"I shall never surrender or retreat," Travis said. "I call on you in the name of liberty, of patriotism, and everything dear to the American character to come to our aid." He would hold out, said Travis, as long as he could. He signed the letter, "Victory or death."

We thought that the letter had been answered by troops led by a man named Fannin. Until we received a second letter, we did not know that Fannin had failed Travis.

When the second letter arrived, we were sitting in a convention that would decide the fate of Texas. Robert Potter rose and moved that the convention should be stopped and that all the men there should get their guns and march to the Alamo.

All eyes were turned on me as I rose from my seat. I said that Potter's suggestion was madness. I told them we had, to be sure, said that we were independent, but that we had no government. If we left the convention, we would never have a government. The very thing Travis was fighting for would be lost.

I spoke for nearly an hour. I told them that I would go myself to help the brave men of the Alamo. I stopped speaking and, in less than an hour, I was on my battle-horse and, with three or four friends, was on my way to the Alamo.

We were too late. At the very moment I was speaking in the convention, those brave men were meeting their fate. But another time would come—and another outcome.

On April 21, 1836, at San Jacinto we engaged Santa Anna in battle. Our cry was, "Remember the Alamo!" We were victorious.

Toward evening of the next day, Santa Anna was brought to me. He asked why I had waited to attack, knowing that he had reinforcements coming.

"It matters not how many reinforcements you may have, sir," I said. Then I took from my pocket an ear of dry corn, partly eaten. "Do you ever expect to conquer men who fight for freedom when their general can march four days with one ear of corn for his rations?"

Some of my soldiers gathered around and asked for the corn, to plant it. "We'll call it Houston corn," they said, but I told them to call it San Jacinto corn, to remind them of their bravery.

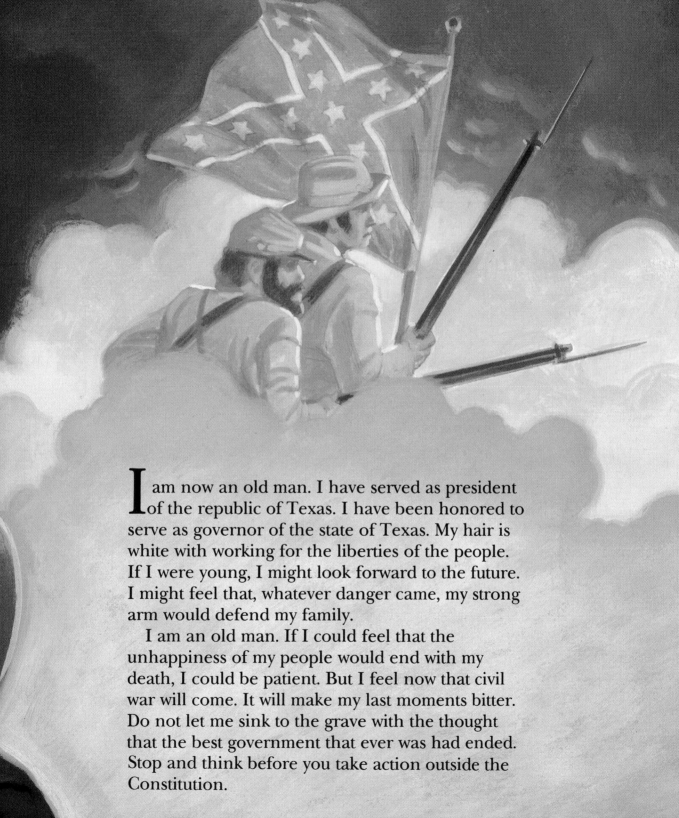

I am now an old man. I have served as president of the republic of Texas. I have been honored to serve as governor of the state of Texas. My hair is white with working for the liberties of the people. If I were young, I might look forward to the future. I might feel that, whatever danger came, my strong arm would defend my family.

I am an old man. If I could feel that the unhappiness of my people would end with my death, I could be patient. But I feel now that civil war will come. It will make my last moments bitter. Do not let me sink to the grave with the thought that the best government that ever was had ended. Stop and think before you take action outside the Constitution.

Sam Houston could not stop the Civil War. He could not keep Texas out of it. And he died before he could see the Union whole again.